Half Century

Raymond Evans was born in industrial South-East Wales in 1944, a few months before the D-Day landings and migrated with his parents to Australia in 1948–49. He is best known as an Australian social historian, widely published in such fields as race relations, convict studies, war and society study, gender relations and popular culture. His writings include *Exclusion, Exploitation and Extermination*, *Loyalty and Disloyalty*, *The Red Flag Riots*, *Gender Relations in Australia*, *1901: Our Future's Past*, *Fighting Words*, *Radical Brisbane* and *A History of Queensland*. This volume, which covers roughly fifty years of his life, is his first foray into poetry.

Raymond Evans

Half Century

Fifty Poems, Personal and Political

Half Century: Fifty Poems, Personal and Political
ISBN 978 1 76041 413 9
Copyright © Raymond Evans 2017

First published 2017 by
GINNINDERRA PRESS
PO Box 3461 Port Adelaide 5015 Australia
www.ginninderrapress.com.au

Contents

Quest	7
3 April 1944	8
Couplet for Mid-century	10
Childhood	11
Evening	14
Fellow Travellers	15
The Old Country	19
The 1950s	22
Plaything	24
On First Hearing Charles Trenet	26
Along Barnett Road	28
Almost Grown	34
Garden Song	36
Australian Childhood	38
Tarzan Gestures Hypnotically	40
Wet Dream Girl	44
Music Time	50
Incongruity	56
After Childhood	58
Seduction	60
Simpson's Road (Bardon, 1963)	62
Spectator (Civil Rights, 1963)	66
Meeting (1966)	68
Blind Girl	69
On First Viewing *La Strada* (1966)	70
In the Primitif	71
Jazz Party – Drawn and Quartered	72
On Writing Erotica	76
Tumescence	78
Strange Confrontation	80

Blockage	82
Adjustment to Reality	84
On That Particular Day	86
Death of Bertrand Russell	91
At State Archives (William Street)	92
Antiquated	100
Easter Incident	103
Extermination	105
Lovers we are then	107
Evil Landscape	108
All I remember	109
Sydney Excursion	110
Raw Pleasure	111
For Mike Parr	112
Remembrance	113
Song for 2012 in four-part harmony	119
Wantime Street	123
Assignation	127
On Meeting You	130
If I Lay Naked	132

Quest

Where is that place beneath
the sleeping stones, the sealed waters,
the settled leaves

I need to find:
To turn the leaf, part the waters,
raise the stone.

Enter that place,
brushing fernlike now and then
the flimsy cloth of my back.

A place unfound,
underground, moss-whispering
between knuckled roots.

A place
of fathomed splendour; caverned joy.
That unreal place

ungrasped:
A reach away, unreached,
unentered, unseen…

far away.
A calling tunnel in my mind,
ever close.

3 April 1944

On the day that I was born,
somewhere a bell was ringing.
There were Angels dining at the Ritz
and Vera Lynn was singing.

On the day that I was born,
people turned aside and shivered
at icy winds blown from the east
and telegrams delivered.

On the day that I was born,
the windows all were blacked.
National Velvet was on release
and the cinemas were packed.

On the day that I was born,
there were rations on each table.
Armed servicemen kept staring
at the legs of Betty Grable.

On the evening I was born,
bombs dropped on towns nearby.
There were sirens briefly blaring
and searchlights in the sky.

On the evening I was born,
they formed another all-Welsh choir.
Glenn Miller had gone missing,
shot down by friendly fire.

On the evening I was born,
'Stardust' was on the hit parade.
And Uncle George was flying
on a German bombing raid.

On the day that I was born,
all was quiet in Tel Aviv.
Anne Frank and Adolf Hitler
had little time to live.

The day that I was born,
marked my Granddad's birth as well.
His body carried shrapnel
from the Battle of Fromelles.

On the night that I was born,
my mother nearly died.
At the Merthyr Tydfil Workhouse
I took in a breath and cried.

'Will you stop that blasted crying!'
I then heard someone shout,
'Or we will give you something
to really cry about.'

Couplet for Mid-century

'I saw eternity the other night':
Ezra Pound in a cage of light.

Childhood

(Merthyr Tydfil, 1947)

I

The man with the wonky glass eye
winks at the woman
with the white elephant leg.
Awkwardly, they dance
towards me –
just a little boy
after all!

I run to the window ledge,
past the tattered pouffe;
Chick's Own and *Tiny Tots*
poking awkwardly out
like lettuce in a bun.

And, of course,
the smelly pot
in a corner of
this damp, yellowing room –
And stand squarely there,
at the frayed curtain
head down
so as not to see,
keeping guard over
my tiny herd
of shiny metal animals.

II

The mottled rocking horse
I would not ride
when I was small
was grinning in the kitchen;
its mad rolled eye
cocked to festoons of flypaper,
rich in fly-currants.

I will not touch
the musty, busted golliwog
with black worm-hair,
stuffed behind books
in the cupboard by the scullery;
or even put my hand
into that shelf.
It watches every time
I take a book.
And the doors sway slightly open
after I shut them.
(I know it gently pushes them
with a sickly arm.)

'It's not alive. Come here. Touch it,'
they say, but
I know differently
and cry and run.
It is the only way.

It lies unclean, limp and dead
and never moves its eye
when they look in.

But one night
it might
come flopping up the stairs
between its long, stuffed arms
and onto the bed
where I am lying,
and trying
to beguile the princess.

Evening

I

The black ape
of night
swung down the sky.

Its long toes
entered the earth
and uprooted the moon.

II

The moon:
blond grape
wrung clean
of star seeds.

The sun:
crisp coin
slipped golden
into the brazen bank of the sea.

The earth:
blind mole
burrowing circular
its cold, velvet tunnel.

Fellow Travellers

We smelt Australia
well before we saw it:
The scent of baked land
on a warm sea breeze
that night in 1949,
just after the old year passed.
It assailed the nostrils,
much as the smell of lucerne,
with horse underneath it,
assails,
as one approaches a barn.
Smelling of hope and fear.
It said to my father,
'I may be lucky
but I will certainly
be tough.'
He hunched at the ship's rail,
recalling the snows of '47
towering above the train
and that blasted shovel,
frozen in his hand –
the mountain ponies coming down
into the cobbled streets,
more cold than cautious.

But home nevertheless.

He thought of bananas
and beaches:
'A Land Without Winter'.
His hands gripped
the warm railing
like a talisman.
Too anxious for sleep,
he talked and laughed
with an Indian crew hand
to keep his courage up.

In our segregated cabin,
as HMS *Somersetshire*
banked and rolled,
my mother was
back where she once was
and remembered
the place that she smelled,
hoping it had changed
for the better since the last time:
that Great Depression
of utter hopelessness;
and of the great Dalmatian
freckles
it had burnt
into her skin,
marking her
as the schoolyard
freak
back home in Merthyr.

And I,
cocooned within
the moment,
lie like an inert pupae
in my narrow bunk,
idly wondering
what 'Australia' means;
and if I might see
a platypus tomorrow.

The next day
we walked out
onto the anvil
of this land;
and for the first time
felt its crust
beneath our feet.
The sun was there
to greet us,
and the butterflies landing,
even though we were
penniless as refugees.
We walked Fremantle,
too poor for
the train to Perth,
peering into shops,
'Can I help you?'
'No thank you.
We are only looking.'

'Don't be a drongo,'
we overheard someone say.
A drongo is
something not to be
here.

Uncle Joe,
no longer a Dambuster,
came back with ice creams
for all –
the biggest I had ever seen.

I sat at the railway siding,
looking up at the great
azure bowl of the sky,
licking my first taste
of Australia,
feeling a stone in my sandal.
The ice cream
ran down my wrist.
A mosquito landed on my arm.
'You are getting burnt,'
my mother said.

The Old Country

'Back home in the Old Country,'
my mother'd always say,
'the fish and chips were better
on any given day.

You'd come out of the Castle
and the latest double bill.
The sky'd be filled with snowflakes
and the air all crisp and chill.

You'd know just what you wanted.
You were in without a halt,
"Two slabs of hake, six penn'oth of chips
with vinegar and salt."

You'd get a lot for sixpence.
You'd feel you'd had a win.
"Fish with a chip on its shoulder,"
Thomas the Fish would grin.

You'd clutch the package to you,
all warm against your chest;
with friendly voices calling,
"*Nostar!*" and "All the Best!"

The snow'd be swiftly falling
as you'd come in the front door.
A fire burning in the grate;
the dog upon the floor.

You'd open up the packet.
A heap of golden brown –
the room would smell delicious.
Nan'd smile and say, "Sit down!"

You'd eat it with your fingers.
No need for knife and fork.
You were so busy chewing,
there'd be no time for talk.

The chips were always perfect.
The hake was gleaming white,
with a pile of bread and butter
on a cold and frosty night.

You'd eat a good half hour
till you felt that you might burst.
You'd eat it from the paper
with tea to quench your thirst.

But out here in Australia,
they've got no idea of that.
The fish is dark and oily.
The chips are full of fat.

Out here the fish-shop people
are rough as guts and rude.
The humidity is terrible.
It puts you off your food.

The people back in Merthyr
run rings around these Aussies.
Even in the backyard there
you'll be eaten up by mozzies.

So I'd rather be in Merthyr
for all its poverty
than living here in Bardon,
trapped in Tombstone Territory.'

As her diatribe continued,
Dad's face betrayed despair;
until at last he ventured,
'Are you being entirely fair?'

'Not being fair!' Mam thundered,
rising sharply from her place
and coming round the table
to confront him face to face,

'This whole country is barbaric
from Cape York to Ballarat.
So don't talk to me of fairness!
Now I'm going to feed the cat.'

The 1950s

A road going nowhere –
that goes on into grass –
is the road that I love.
A path disappearing
around a corner
in a bright wood.
A stairway ending,
going upward
into blueness.
A creek where no one goes.

Through a hole
in the broken fence
and into the lantana bushes,
along a narrow track,
hidden and shaded,
made before bitumen,
before the horses came,
before guns;
and into the cicada roar.

To where we get the clay
and flinty shale
or catch the yabbies
or lie on warm ground
or make the spears
and build cubbies,
or roll down green hillsides,
calling the dogs to us
and singing our rollicking songs.

When we were pirates
or savages
or cut-throats
or Beagle Boys;
or rascals
or Musketeers;
escaped convicts
or lion tamers –
or broken men
just back from the war
and safe in our homeland again.

Plaything

'Noela Pitts
has nits,'
tomorrow's respectable citizens sang
in clean shorts and sandals
and cruel, chanting teams
at school.

Daily,
gaily,
everyone taunted
the face mucous ugly
and limbs lightly tainted
with faint violet rosettes.

Scoring and bruising
with the label of leper,
we ambushed her misery
and socks rolling grimy
down under her ankles
in every dark corner.

To be pushed upon her
held all the revulsion
of cuddling vermin.
I could no more touch her
than the soiled piles of bandage
we saw at the dump.

An alert gang of playmates
one day claimed for certain
her bottom was naked.
So quick hands went grabbing,
risking contagion,
at her ragged hems.

In wretched defence of
her small, puckered groin,
she hurled herself at them
as they darted and tugged her
and foamed she would give them
her terrible plague –

her mythical plague.

Flailing in anguish
she screamed her hate at us,
her voice wrestling with phlegm.
Until that moment
I had not seen her weeping
nor the scars we had branded.

It was too easy to wish then
I had just once said,
'Leave her alone.'

Reminiscing years later
Someone said laughing,
'Noela Pitts you should see now –

Old Saggy Tits!'
and 'What hell we gave her'
was still all I could say.

On First Hearing Charles Trenet

I sit amidst the cooking smells
on the stool my father made;
and the wireless is playing
its hypnotic serenade.

On the laminex my homework lies.
The peas have all been shelled.
The parting cries of passers-by
have nearly all been yelled.

I inhabit my small corner
down by the bakelite;
and the music from the radio
befriends the lonely night.

Then through the darkness ripple
the first verses of 'La Mer'.
An electric charge runs through me
to the tip of every hair.

The voice is like a swooping bird.
The melody's a swelling tide;
and I am cast adrift on it,
all anchorless and mystified.

The kitchen walls are towering waves.
The kitchen floor is yellow sand.
My tiny stool's a mighty raft.
A seagull perches on my hand.

The salt air still caresses
as my mother sets the tea;
and a French voice now possesses
every particle of me.

Along Barnett Road

On some ancient '50s day,
shiny as wet pebbles
in the sunlight,
we exploded red bungers,
big as saveloys,
in the letter boxes
of Barnett Road,
marvelling
at the grandeur
of their tinny eruptions;
and running for the lantana
when the yelling began.

Weighing spuds
in five-pound bags
beneath the floor
and customers' feet
in McMahon's General Store,
we'd found
another bag of antique crackers
from some forgotten Guy Fawkes,
years before:
faded Tom Thumb strings,
packs of sparklers
losing their sparkle
and other dubious things…
But the bungers were still good.

'You kids can have 'em,'
Old McMahon had said,
'I was going to give youse pocket money;
but they can be your pay instead.'

We'd scared Ronnie Richards'
cocker spaniel
and Auntie Lucy's
tortoiseshell
as well as,
on the day before,
Mr and Mrs Ritzinn,
who'd slipped quietly in
after the war.
She'd shown me
a number on her stencilled arm,
brushing aside the flour
as she baked
at her kitchen oven.
'It didn't happen here,' she cried,
'It was over there.
Bad people. Germans!'
'It's a big number,' I'd replied.

All along Barnett Road,
that dusty, rutted way,
we were the Three Musketeers,
Harvey, Graham and I,
as we sauntered about

after pikelets and Rosella jam,
kicking up the dust;
our tanned faces
practicing yawning perhaps
or making fish lips,
with umbrella-tree sabres
under our belts,
incendiaries in our pockets,
our fingers on the pulse
of the place.
Houses down one side;
bushland the other –
a mountain and a creek
that was our own.

In wheeled Jimmy Moore,
his black jacket unzipped,
a love bite on his neck:
Bardon's bona fide Bodgie.
'As rough as guts,'
neighbours would roar
above his motorbike din,
popping and snapping
like our Tom Thumb strings.
We followed him in.

He lifted big Brando boots
onto the bed,
crumpled notes and shiny coins –
florins and shillings –
in a careless heap
on the bedside stand.
And beneath, in mint condition,
neatly stacked,
a good three-foot pile:
a taboo trove of
Man monthlies,
the odd *Pocket Man*,
and the even
punier *Man Junior*.

For a time
he'd let us rifle through them,
gazing at the alabaster nudes,
smooth as Greek statues.
Graham paused at a spread:
American Indians shot down
by US Cavalry.
But these were all black
and Aboriginal instead.
'This didn't happen here…
It couldn't have…' Graham said.

'Fuckin' cops man!' snarled Jimmy
over his head.
'No way!' we near-whispered.
Our eyes took in the dead.

Then 'BANG!' he yelled,
slapping an open palm
onto the page,
laughing as we jumped
like Auntie Lucy's cat.
'That's what happened, gents:
they had it all –'
(gesturing to the eucalypts
across the road)
'Then BANG! BANG! BANG!'
(pointing a yellowed finger
at each in turn)
'Just like that:
Fuckin' fireworks all right:
Much louder than your bloody cracker night!
They lost the lot
and they were gone…
a long, long time ago –
Australia went from black to white
and then everything moved on.
Where the fuck d'youse think they went?'

In an awkward silence
we stood like dumbstruck fools.
We'd never thought of violence.
It wasn't taught in schools.

No one spoke
till Jimmy,
scooping up some silver
and shutting up the *Man*,
changed tack and said,
'Hey! Forget all that.
Now here's the plan:
Just got me pay –
so how's about three bubblegums
if youse'll go and get
a large bottle of sarse for us
up at McMahon's Store –
and a pack of Craven A.
Just tell 'em they're for Jimmy Moore.
But if they start getting skitterish
over the ciggies
and makin' the usual fuss,
just get some
Nigger Boy Liquorice.
That'll do the four of us.'

Almost Grown

Walking backward
up Outlook Crescent
without falling over;
spinning with eyes closed
under a bulbous moon
by the camellia bushes;
skipping along the dirt road
through westerly winds
to school;
staying up on tiptoes
all the way
to the tram terminus;
jumping sideways
to miss the lightning strike.
Keeping my wits about me.

But NEVERTHELESS:
tumbling down a flight of stairs
onto cold concrete;
getting skittled
by some errant pushbike rider;
catching a cricket ball
between the eyes
on the school oval;
opening my knee
to the white bone,
cutting lantana
with a cane knife;
getting stuck up a tree
opposite the barber's
under a blazing sun.
Not watching what I am doing.

And not forgetting:
The tinea between my toes;
the fat leech between my toes;
the grey tick inside my navel;
the bee sting closing my right eye;
the spider bite inflating my penis
like a toy balloon;
a circus calf bite
from a Shetland pony.
While trying to be more careful.

But then again:
a bold girl named Carol
smiling down at me
through the Grade Four window;
and Dale, dark and wild,
wrestling me silently
behind the teacher's back;
Janice explaining
'fucking' after school;
laughing Lorraine,
parting her smooth
brown legs above me;
and Joyce,
with her generous smile,
kissing me like Maureen O'Hara.
Learning something new each day.

Garden Song

Old Mrs Moses,
under cauliflower skies,
pruned new roses
to commensurate size.

Her earth,
caked Christmas-rich
and raisin-rocked,
she sliced and turfed
and petal-iced,
by concrete gnomes,
in worn blue socks.

Under her hat,
straw-baked
and crisp sun-cracked,
she dug
with green fork
into pudding loam:
Her hands,
pink-rubbered,
smeared with slug.

She smiled
with her garden
on bead-curtain rain;
and bold by
her crying window,
she opened and flowered

to a grey
overcoat lover,
the gunpowder cloud.

Bent varicosed legs,
held firm to earth
by sandalled toes,
her thatched head
tossed in wind
with fresh blooms,
nodding round
the tadpole pools.

Plump, rosy
pumpkin among roses,
she trowelled her flowers
to bloom unplucked
and shout their splendours
at her brown serge;
and for their seeds
she dreamed all the lovers
sown young
into the black earth.

Australian Childhood

Bardon, 1950s

I   Earth

The hill there,
a jelly
of dancing grasses:
the ruffled coat
of the green beast's back
we'll ride,
astride
a chequered picnic saddle,
to the flood-pink land
behind our eyes.

Warm-furred and lazy,
the wombat hill
ripples and chuckles
in its fat emerald dream.

II   Water

In the bulrush days,
on our shale-rocked, shallow creek,
we'd launch tin canoes –
rippling roof fragments,
ripped and dinted
and warped in a pod.

Hand-paddling
on damp, gravelled knees,
we'd glide and jar
through bird screams,
eel-vines
and bearded weeds.

Graham,
so sure and sharp,
brown Indian-faced,
steady-wobbling
ahead.

I,
small and white,
scrub-freckled,
frightened,
lurching behind.

Grinding on
slimy stones,
dribbling down
ribbon-slopes,
to five o'clock.

Tarzan Gestures Hypnotically

One morning
when I was ten,
Tarzan gestured to me,
hypnotically.
Or,
more specifically,
from a bookstand way back then,
Tarzan and the Ant Men.

Tarzan wore his loincloth red.
The Ant Men rode their mini-impala.
I wore galoshes and sou'wester,
pulled down like a balaclava,
as I strode up Bulcock Street:
sloshing along in grey, soggy plastic
to the papershop
up Pumistone Hill,
hoping no girl would notice me,
looking 'such a spastic' –
as the rain slanted down
on our last precious days
at Harmony Flats,
Caloundra Town.

'No comics today,' Dad had said.
'Get something that will last instead…'
(Gesturing to the tall, revolving racks
of paperbacks
by the dim newsagent's door.)
'Like old Tarzan here…
What about
Tarzan at the Earth's Core?
Or,
try this one then,
Tarzan and the Ant Men.

Two shillings and sixpence
was all I had,
so things grew rapidly tense.
Then, in Cousin Harvey went
with *Tarzan the Magnificent*.
The African sun
baked Tarzan's broad flanks
as, without hint of fear,
he faced
the massed impala ranks.
Each Ant Man waved his tiny spear.

I trudged back
under leaden skies
with Tarzan tucked inside my mac,
though still unsure
of my expensive prize.
The print, after all,
a mere ant track;
and names of Russian literary guise,
larger than an Ant Man's size:
Trohanadalmakus;
Zertalacolon;
Veltoptismakus
and so on.

By evening,
rain still pounding hard outside,
Harvey cast his tome aside.
Alone, I soldiered on,
ignoring nagging bookish troubles
and Harvey lamely laughing now
at 'Edgar Rice Bubbles'.
The flight of Ska the Vulture
spurred me on.

Next morning,
with sun returning,
our hearts singing
and backs slowly burning,
we took once more
to shell-hunting
and beach racing,
Catherine wheels
and seagull chasing;
while, near at hand,
Ska the Vulture
And Tarzan, Ape Man,
Lay in silent waiting
On my chipped,
enamel-green
nightstand.

Wet Dream Girl

Once again:
rain on the banana leaves
and slanting across
the dark, pebbled windows
with the elephant-head clasps.

I trust its persistence.
Against the fronds
it drums on:
interminable.
It may come down
like this all night;
and I am held
inside that sound,
encased within
the walls of the drum
that beats above
and around me.

I know exactly where I am.
I am not in this narrow bed.
I am not in these striped pyjamas.
I am not even fourteen at present.
I can be where I want.
You will marvel
when I tell you
where I really am.

I am
on a vast and desolate plain.
An icy, biting wind
whips the rain in swirling torrents.
For miles around
nothing can be seen
save the outline of my tent,
my magical tent
that keeps me dry and warm
and contented.
As safe as houses.
My lantern shines out,
yellow and pale,
into a pitch-dark night.

Rain continuing,
but now harder.
Soon this bulging tarpaulin
above me,
I know,
will begin to drip:
a mere touch will do it –
and how, on earth,
am I able to keep
so dry and warm
on this cold, damp earth?
Perhaps I am not in a tent
at all.

Perhaps —
and this now seems entirely feasible —

it is more of
a yurt.
A sturdy yurt on the vast and desolate plain:
solid, weatherproofed
and geodesic.
Yes,
of course it is.
I've always fancied a yurt.

Driving rain
thuds against its impervious hide
as I remain bone dry inside:
I can even stand and walk around
in here;
and there is a small,
efficient stove for heating.
Furs and hides,
cushions, doonas and eiderdowns
blanket the rough pine floor.
My shaggy wolfhound,
Gruff,
hunkers obediently down
in his corner —
Or rather,
in his special place —
as yurts
don't have corners.

Each of us
bends to his bowl
of hot, nutritious food
from a bubbling pot.
Then Gruff looks up
and quietly growls.
Above the teeming rain
an urgent scraping
against the yurt's outer wall.
A wild animal, perhaps?
A wounded lynx?
A bold ocelot?
Another bloody capybara?

Out there:
the deep black of night,
low, scudding clouds
and endless downpour.
Cautiously,
I lower the flap
and peer out,
one hand tightly grips
Gruff's collar.

And, of course,
it is the bent figure
of a young woman
(No big surprises here!)
one frozen hand on the slick
yurt wall
to hold her upright.
Shaking…weak…bedraggled…
can hardly speak
above the pounding din…

'Lost' is all she whispers
and stumbles in.

So now we are three:
Gruff, this girl and me…

Frozen, shivering still
and eternally grateful,
she sheds sodden clothing
as I face the stove
to get something warm
into her as fast as possible.
There is nowhere else to go.

As I turn,
she is drawing an ample fur
around her slim, white body.
Her lank hair
is drying in the warmth:
a rich, golden brown.
She reaches earnestly for the bowl,
her dark eyes cast down.
I plan getting to know her well.

And she will stay
so close our breaths now mingle,
as long as this night,
and the rain,
pelting hard on the banana suckers,
lasts.

Music Time

I Runaway Bus

I have been on this busted old bus,
rusty and encrusted,
for some time now.
Al Jolson in black face
was still driving
when I climbed on
back then;
and Hank Williams coughing
up his lung on the long back seat.
Everyone else happily humming,
'Sparrow in the treetop'…
Until one day, near Rockdale,
some teens jumped in
yelling, 'Everybody
Razzle-Dazzle!'
No one really got it;
so they slashed the vinyl
seat covers for fun.
The ride certainly got
bumpier from then on.
The new, sloe-eyed,
moon-faced bus driver
wasn't much help either
in calming things down.

II Four o'Clock Rock

The spine of this house
is a fibro corridor
of seven doors,
before the door
to my room –
A floor of cold lino,
lime green;
walls of avocado;
an off-white ceiling.

There is nothing
auspicious about it.
It is simply a throughway
from back-door to bedroom.
You go down and up it
or duck into another room.
It is for such movements only,
not rest or discovery…
though Dad taught me to box
and bowl here
with an old tennis ball –
You do not sit or eat
here
or sleep, wash or defecate
as you might in other rooms.
You do not read
or play the wireless
or study and dream.

In fact
you hold only
the merest of passing conversations.

So, this day,
high school being over,
I pass down it as usual
with my brown port,
full of dubious knowledge.
In my sister's room,
second door on the left,
a small, chocolate radio
plays on the lowboy...
Without thinking of anything
in particular
in that empty passageway –
maybe trigonometry
or a girl on the tram –
and expecting nothing much
immediately
beyond homework
and a predictable dinner...
my sister silently colouring in
my mother peeling potatoes in the kitchen...

But
the radio loudly plays
and a sound detonates
simultaneously
in my ears, chest
and brain,
blowing thought aside.
In this moment,
in that narrow corridor,
I am being changed utterly,
(as Yeats would say).
I stop in my tracks
holding the heavy port,
transfixed for minutes
in time and place.

It is August 1958.
I am hearing rock'n'roll
in an Australian vernacular.
I am hearing Johnny O'Keefe
out of Sydney.
I am hearing the Deejays
playing 'So Tough'.

I am not quite sure yet
what I am hearing.
But something is afoot here.
Something is percolating.
Something
new in this house,
in this tiny passage,
that will change
everything
here and now
in me
from now on.
Something that is no longer
half-arsed.
Something that pounds
and pounds from the radio
like my heart pounds.

Something that is rolling
down the spine of this house
like a westerly wind.
Did the floor move just then?
Is the fibro cracking?

It rushes up my spine,
lighting up the synapses.
It opens my mouth
in dumb delight
and lifts up
the goosebump on my arms –
and all that is inside me
is now trying
to break out.

In the precise moment
of those eight syllables
of 'tough',
projecting from that raw throat,
I know
I have crossed
some invisible line
on the green lino;
something wild has barged in
through a side door;
and I shall never be
quite the same
quiet being again.

Incongruity

Imelda,
old maid,
dodging elephant trunks,
spindled between dungheaps
in cobble-black boots
at the circus.

Reeling from lions' smell,
lace 'kerchief to nose.
Through the ring of their roar
a stallion cantered
between the rude thighs
of a straddling girl,
riding breasts doved
in wet, silk pink.

Black crepe on rainbow canvas,
Imelda felt
a tightening
of her walnut chest
as she brushed
the peeling wagon paint –
cage after cage of sad performers,
tamed with crisp brutality.

Sickening now,
she sat
by hot hay bales,
her buttock bones
chiselling the hardwood bench –
tugged lightly
a single, silver strand
of hay in her chin.
Metal music dinned her ears
and laughter floated
from within.

Rising unsteadily,
she tutted home
to her mahogany cat.

After Childhood

I Walk after Rain (Bardon, 1960)

Wings of newsprint,
like freckled, frightened geese,
skid the wind-soaked street;
And I,
to my trudging feet,
feel their crackle on gravel.

Wrapped in my bear-brown coat.
The wind's white teeth
at my bare face;
the smell of past rain
in my nostrils,
I press on.

Beyond the cutting,
at the park,
among eucalypts,
lank and dripping,
I bend
to sail a black twig ship
by talonned roots
and brown, wet sparrows,
and be the blood-kneed boy again.

II Later still

It has been so long
since the flame-flower –
a crest of blood –
sang on the white paling,
crying, 'Live!
Bleeding glorious
each drop of sun-blood
into the singing-sun whiteness...'

And the day
I could vein the essence
of leaves in my pores,
in my sweet tree limbs,
bleeding the white sap
through my red-blood bones:
and catch
a reeling sense of skin
beneath the rapture of my knuckles.

Seduction

Towards dusk,
a bold, long-toed girl
on a wobbly bike
entices me.

Pink rubber grips on
silver handlebars
almost graze her nipples,
swelling like lozenges
as they're sucked.

Beneath her bright
and tiny top,
her breasts so small,
they do not move
as the bicycle wobbles.

She doubles me
to the creek,
throwing down her bike
on some lush, emerald spot.

Leans against
a eucalypt,
the sole of a bare foot
upon the smooth bark.

Hitching up a loose skirt
over brown legs, smiles and says:
'I am a wench.
Do you like wenches?'

Looking down at the grass,
says, 'It is wet,'
tracing an arc of dirt
with a long toe.

A tongue
is clearly visible
inside her yellow panties.
'Let us take everything off,'
she says.

And I was merely
minding my own business,
on my way
to the youth club.

Afterwards,
pedalling away,
she rings her bell,
two chirrupy rasps,
cheerily calling,
'See you round!'
over her shoulder.

So what has transpired here?
It is April.
I am just turned sixteen.
And curious as to how,
by this shallow creek,
the 60s have just breezed in.

Simpson's Road (Bardon, 1963)

Pete Seeger came by today;
or rather went past
across our white bridge,
chasing down a sturdy log
from the Mt Coot-tha roadside
to chop up in town tonight,
singing 'Go Down Old Hannah'
or maybe 'John Henry'
on stage…

Gwen Foster once passed here too
with Bill Harwood –
her dream lion –
laughing at the name 'Wittgenstein'.
'There is no such person!'
she protested like a coquette.
Another war had just ended
and she was not a poet yet.

And quite regularly,
before they laid the bitumen,
a group of three
strolling up the wooded hill,
lost in conversation:

Ernie Lane – his brother off in Paraguay –
exercising his elastic mind and stride;
Arthur Yewen – founder of Socialist Leagues
in London and Sydney
with William Morris and William Morris Hughes –
his one shirt buttoned
over a weakly chest;
and Henry Lawson –
'Joe Swallow' himself –
probably out-distancing a hangover,
a long poem, 'The Cambaroora Star',
burning a hole in his pocket…

Off into the William Taylor hills
to talk politics and poetics – what else? –
along this old bush road,
winding past the one house here
set back from the creek
where Thomas Ryan,
(whom you probably haven't heard of yet)
who will up ahead
first suggest an Anzac Day
for Queensland,
for Australia,
chopping kindling for the copper,
looks up at their chatter
and maybe waves…

And while here,
we had best acknowledge
the original owners,
the Turrbal People,
foraging through these foothills
aeons before Simpson's Road;
and Eulope's five hundred dark warriors
going down in battle
before Moppy's seven hundred
at Mt Coot-tha's base:
and the remnants rounded up
at Cobbler's Flat
and taken away
when the Bardon Estate began
during Ryan's war...

And, of course, all the young Americans,
disorientated, naturally enough,
crossing the bridge in convoys,
en route to the largest ammunition dump
in the Southern Hemisphere
at the well-named Slaughter Falls
as the Japs made their advance
during the subsequent conflagration.

And then, later
this other trio:
three small boys,
climbing the familiar hill –
going up Simpson's Road,
that well-known gradient,
together for the umpteenth time,
past Ryan's old house,
its yard now overgrown…

Past the crumbling horse-trough
and the Infants School;
past the unknown places
where Lane and Yewen,
squatting down on stumps,
first heard Lawson's dark imagery
of hunted 'Chinkies';
where the Yanks had counted out their days;
where Harwood had mocked 'Wittgenstein';
where Seeger would find his log;
where the Turrbal had camped
and hunted and fought and danced…

With not a clue in our airy heads,
full of cicada drone,
about any of that:
three active little minds,
congested with joy
and fixed upon Hollywood, kites and lollies.

Spectator (Civil Rights, 1963)

As I went down
to our town square,
black people sitting
everywhere.

How ungodly
I declare.
Clean white town
with black folk there –
chanting,
clapping,
black thigh slapping.
Police dogs yapping.
Dusty air.
Agitating,
integrating.
Gleaming sweat
through kinky hair.

Makes me nervous.
Makes me sick.
Want to vomit.
Want to kick.
God, I swear
they want our women,
bawling, 'Freedom!',
not quite human.
Rubber lips
and juice to spare.

Nigger naked
under clothing.
Massive hatred,
passive loathing.
Squatting ape-like,
jelly-rolling.
Funky smell
and tunneled noses:
Make them dance
with prods and hoses.
Need a brick
or need a hammer.
Smash the mouths
that yell and yammer.

This fine day
in Alabama.

Meeting (1966)

Unloved in my unlovely days:
your hair
a lost sweep
of broken chords.

Came to my pine cage
of ice light,
sunless,
sudden-eyed.

Tracing
your questing tongue
over the glacial ache
within me.

Warm, moth-wet flutter
lacing my chest;
caged in our wonder
of soft hair and calm.

Blind Girl

Chalk bright by grey tides,
I caught
a white-wand body,
thin and gentle at dusk,
upon an open shore.
The grey tides running:
The sigh and hiss
on cold sand.

This lone, nude body
wading, lowering at sea edge;
and once kitten-batting water
in cautious abandon.

Caught awkward a moment
on one taut thigh –
left foot inward-turning,
then graceful, heron-child dipping,
gliding unfeathered flesh into
pale, salt cream.

Wind-whipped nipple points;
nervous hair sweeping
and nesting her hidden,
unseeing milk eyes.

On First Viewing *La Strada* (1966)

'Gelsomina!'
The name sang.
The moon-white
moonstone rang
on tin.
The drum –
a clumsy staccato.
The odd noise;
the odd face.
The nipple-tipped nose.
The abashed,
eyelashed eyes.
A mouth of
soft, trembling rubber.

The sad eyes swell
and scan
the beach; the tree;
the old horse;
the stone step; the sheep;
the worn blanket coat;
the stick and the trumpet.

In the Primitif

on first seeing Mike Parr – early 1966

A girl drew nude-girl
and her stump-arm boy
spoke with passion
of colour and line;
and his stump hung
like sausage from sleeve,
or jerked up like
some signal
or a penguin wing.

Her hair
shone across her back:
A golden spaniel –
and Les said
we'd wear
our hair like that
if we were girls.

His one hand
spanned and stroked her thigh,
blue-and-white checked,
held between the two
perfectly good legs
that he had;
as she stroked the nude buttock
of the girl she drew
with shading pencil.

Jazz Party – Drawn and Quartered

I

Smoke:
pale, stale
frail horses,
sidling up
from cigarette straw.
Pale horses sigh,
pale horses cry
and scrape a hoof
along cold wall,
against grey roof.

Out of blackness,
on feet of shadow,
Septimus stood
in his cage of blood,
his flesh and sang.
(Tangled now,
I am
pierced by trumpets'
screaming swords.)
Sally slue-foots
soapy cement
while Roger,
Jolly Roger,
slow thinking,
drinking blind,
rapes her in
the bushes of his mind.

II

Down, down,
Piltdown men
to the loins of your women
prowling before you.
Their voices kining,
howling, whine
a claw,
a maw,
a jaw,
roaring in heat:
a jumble of pullovers
holding flesh cannibals;
a splatter of cymbals
and voices smash on the walls.

III

Her body –
a spur,
a spear,
sharded glass;
as I pass
I stare
in fear
metal woman
(brittle common
brutal woman)
your heart
of hair
a snare
you open,
petal woman,
to stroke and tear
like a nettle.

IV

Over that floor
Eros is swirling,
hurling
and spilling his phallus
upon soaked heads.
They swim in beer-sperm,
sink, dainty skip:
human lips ready
all over their bodies
to kiss trumpet horns.

Behind yellow brass,
piano gums kick
bucking teeth:

You, beneath,
take my tongue
and hook your splendid,
bended legs
to swallow a drum.

A piece of automatic writing, produced in situ at a University of Queensland Jazz Party in 1966 in the cement basement of the Refectory, at Mike Parr's instigation. The wine and beer flowed. I sat there scribbling this on small cards and the band played on.

On Writing Erotica

Sensual words skating out
onto a frozen page
should stroke and glide
not clatter and thud.
Hover and spin,
not grasp or clump:
languid, dappled words,
shepherding
more brazen ones
out to posture and dance.

Their watchful keeper
releases them
judiciously,
and in good measure;
neither caressing each one
as it slides out
nor losing control
at the last moment
when word becomes flesh.

Such responsibility
for the arousal of strangers –
albeit paying customers –
weighs heavily
on the white page
where any may come,
expectantly,
for release.

But for you,
no release;
beside watching
words falling
hungrily upon
words:
open displays
of cool precision
that you may
order sharply
into line
but never
break ranks
to join.

Up there,
calibrating arousal;
bending over the hot tub,
testing the temperature
with a chaste elbow;
scribbling away
in your cold tower.
And never letting down
your hair.

Tumescence

So much here
that is hard.

All body parts, that is,
pink, purple and white,
readied for action:
Four standing nipples;
Clit, hardening to sharp.
Labia cresting.
Cock upstanding.
Hard teeth and
ferocious pelvis.

But softness too:
soft words,
softly more obscene.
Soft mouths meshing.
Slow tongues
leisurely mounting in turn.
Large, splayed breasts
and soft, composed buttocks.
Vulva, soaked and open.

And all in motion.
Hard finding soft.
Soft seeking hard.

We lock inside –
a perfect fit.
Each tiny movement,
exquisite.

We forego time;
and as we do,
we forego
who is inside who.

It doesn't matter
while it's done.
Two beings busy
being one.

Strange Confrontation

One night last summer,
for some reason,
I woke restless and sat up in bed.
Nothing had changed
but for someone
sitting at my desk in darkness
at the end of the room.
Silently I rose and, coming closer,
was not really surprised
to find it was myself sitting there.
My notes lay open under me;
and I, head on arms,
was slumped across them.

As I reached to shake my shoulder,
someone (I think it was an angel),
held me back and whispered,
'Leave him alone. He is trying to work.'
Of course all this time
I knew I was dreaming.
So, turning, went back to bed.

Later I woke again and saw
I was still sitting there –
but now I had become so old,
for the moon showed distinctly
a gleam of silver hair.
And, as I approached,
I was quite shaken to see
my features warped
and shrunken with age.
My old hand lay
sideways across the page
as if some dried-up claw;
and, in the creases and folds
of the parched skin,
the dust of many years had settled
as I had remained,
motionless,
sleeping there.

Blockage

Sometimes
poems roll out
like gaudy marbles,
bouncing headlong
down stone steps;
or flow like swift streams,
sleek and sandy,
noiselessly, easily;
or even –
when no one is looking –
spill hotly
onto a page:

Haikus shimmering
like sugar-cubes;
sonnets like neat,
gold haystacks;
odes dancing like brolga
in tiny clearings.

But sometimes
words won't come.
But hammer and chatter
in neck and fist,
spin back and shatter
in mixed alphabets,
and won't come.

Nor beauty –
just ground-hogs
(or maybe wart-hogs?)
rooting,
higgledy-piggledy,
the shallows
of my mind,
dumb with blood eyes
and coarse hair.

All else won't come.

Yet, sometimes,
as darkness recedes,
I lie in bed
waiting for my poem
to climb in beside me,
whispering, 'I am here,'
as it runs a cool finger
up my spine.

Adjustment to Reality

Without warning,
it began raining eyeballs.
Down-bouncing,
rolling and bursting,
plopping and bobbing
cod-like in ponds.
Those tufted grass stopped
would not pop
but stared out awry
from green, bushy eyebrows.

And then,
once more,
skies opened and blued
over outside calm.

People's front lawns
gazed back at their watchers,
peering wildly through blinds.
Adults, young and old;
as all round,
dumb and glassy,
eyeballs shone and rolled.

Remember
with pink gloves,
we plucked them in buckets:
the browns, blues and greens,
and learned nothing really
from religion or science,
newspapers or praying,
or Politicos braying,
'More terrorist spies!'
while thrumming,
plum-drumming,
those showers kept coming.

Then at last,
grown accustomed,
yet drawn still by wonder,
with noses to windows,
we beheld falling eyes.

Long ago, that beginning
and these many times after
remain unexplained
and as strange today…
But now I find only
letters complaining
these showers kill squirrels;
and overheard only yesterday,
a young woman saying,
'At night I love lying
and hearing the eyes.'

On That Particular Day

(Vietnam Moratorium, 1970)

Perhaps being older
on that particular day
I was more comfortably back
in the ruck
than these young ones,
eager for the hot, forbidden
asphalt
opening out before them
and the silver tram tracks,
now long buried,
snaking off ahead.

As we had crested the rise,
bunching
at the lights and fruit shop
on Fred Schonell,
I gazed back
down the long aspect of marchers
still winding past the Avalon
from the emptied campus,
the emptied Forum,
where our tinny, insufficient
'Marsellaise',
'All You Need Is Love',
had stepped us out,
minutes before,
laughing at the modernity
of it all.

A whole campus in motion,
or near enough to it,
you might say,
where, years earlier,
thin rivulets of audacity
with our floppy placards
were sucked up into the grey levees.

And out ahead,
turning past the service station
towards Toowong,
long striations of red
and NLF flags,
flying incongruously
beside white peace banners
as in lock step,
probably, as we walked,
other marchers
passing on down
the Ho Chi Minh Trail
on that particular day,
where bicycles were also permitted,
like Burnham Wood
descending on Dunsinane.

While in the city,
as we later heard,
those gathered thinly in the Square
of King George's backward horse
had again thought
that Brisbane,
that string bag and slack-jawed town,
true to form,
would again fail,
as in the south,
thousands effortlessly sat and roared.

But then calling
– as they really did call –
'The Students Are Coming!'
as they had once called,
from that same Square,
'The Wharfies Are Coming!'
during the strife of '48,
as they heard our distant chantings,
shaking the grey Roma Street
buildings,
before they saw us,
like the hosts of Gandalf,
wheeling in.

And after,
as we left the Square
we had over-flown,
I must tell you
the best private moment for us
that no one recorded:
our beautiful friend,
running right out
from her secure job
dusting books in QBD,
dancing almost,
and straight into our arms
and the dole queue
(but not on that particular day).

My pregnant partner and I,
our daughter jogging along inside her,
our beautiful friend beside us,
and others, now lost.

So on we go,
shouting and singing,
past spatters of clapping
and thin lines of boos.
And grim police,
who did not carry
cluster bombs
or Agent Orange
in Brisbane;
down Queen Street
for all to see.
Never such a parade
in this old town –
a small, moving land mass,
tearing itself at last loose
from a continent
of acquiescence and realpolitik,
and making its own uncharted way
into an unknown night
up ahead,
but, shielded in hope back then,
always on towards the sun.

Death of Bertrand Russell

Trying to rise from his bed,
he touched a chord.
He climbed down the chord
and into the street –
dark out at this time
on a clear Welsh night.
People were marching past.
Many (being Welsh) were singing.
Some carried books or placards;
others led animals.
He wondered where they were going…

He watched until they turned the corner,
then slowly walked down the alley
and disappeared through a door.

At State Archives (William Street)

And how am I here
armed only with this biro,
watching the dust motes
dancing up
a golden beam
of afternoon light,
alone at this old, scored table
between long walls
of dark, musty packages,
holding darker secrets
in plain,
brown-paper wrappers,
unopened for generations?

Remembering,
years ago
at Ashgrove
that peculiar charge
of recognition
when drawing for school
those scrolled manuscripts
with their grandly rolled
edges:
The Magna Carta (1215).
The Petition of Right (1628).

Was it merely these
that have brought me
directly down here?
I had no idea
where else to go.
And now,
in every variety
of calligraphy
on these crisp
and fading pages,
day after day,
disclosing
from a time
barely conceivable,
such words as:

*'She died under horrible
circumstances,
having been forgotten
or left designedly
in a paved cell
in complete nudity
for several days.'* (1865)

And…

*'Chinese labourers
beaten with axes
at Homebush Station.'* (1876)

And…

*'A patient
…flogged with a whip
back to his ward.
Several of the inmates
cried out, "Shame."
He is paralysed.'* (1884)

And…

*'I am nearly blind
and may say
friendless.'* (1884)

And…

*'I seen them
chain up a gin
to a tree —
one leg to each side…
for being too long
looking for horses
…the ants were running
all over her person.'* (1892)

And…

I lay down my pen,
gazing
at the lolly-pink
ribbon
festooning
each tan bundle,
straining for
afternoon traffic sounds;
the summer sun
sizzling the asphalt;
a thin breeze
coming up
brisk off the river
behind me;
a footfall,
perhaps,
down the precarious,
circular,
iron stairway;
hand resting
idly on
this old, suspect heap
of unread reports,
filed away
long ago
by the long-dead
for no other eyes
apparently
than mine –

flat, incriminating
little time bombs,
slowly ticking
down.

I glance at my watch:
Three-twenty.
Only another
hour or so
before the tram ride
home and tea.
I take up
the chirpy-yellow biro
and resume:

'*They could not poison them*
or shoot them
or hang them
so they sent them to an island
upon the Pacific
and let them
die there.' (1892)

And…

'*Poor old men,*
50 or 60
years of age,
dying slowly of syphilis.
They held out
their wasted hands,
crying, "Hungry. Hungry,"' (1892)

And…

*'I have shot
13 or 14
niggers in this district
and this is all
the Government has done
for me:
I can't get a bloody nigger
when I want one.
They all go
to the Chinamen.'* (1898)

And…

*'The Russians were showing
their teeth
like wild animals
and dripping saliva.'* (1919)

And…

*'Want any
old hags shot?'* (1920)

(Have you had enough
of this pitiless place yet,
Dear Reader?
I could go on.
I now have filing cabinets
full of
such stuff:

All poetry
of a sort —
indelible missives,
sharp as dog barks.
And nothing,
I would add,
ever done
about any of it.)

Outside,
in William Street,
there was no notice,
that first day,
warning:
'Danger! Keep out!'
as I walked innocently in.
So I am fixated here
for the duration
at the lower level
of Hades
in the oldest building
in the Deep South
of this State,
in the Deep North
of this nation,
exploring at times
the Deeper North
and Wilder West,
caught now
in the rough noose
of Queensland,

– this *'debatable land'*,
 as George Bowen dubbed it –
taking notes
for all I am worth
in these bland
foolscap pads
my mother bought me,
bearing witness daily
before a congregation,
singing lustily, and full of
how well they sing,
with ears and eyes
half-closed.

Antiquated

I A Vision of Army

The army's centipede swords
stride by its side.
The gold dint of helmet caps
limn a sullen glow
above its slow lizard ranks
in scaled, chain-mail skin,
winding up the hill.
Their lances wave
like stubborn crops,
aslant with ribbon banners:
Turkish-red,
Séance-black,
Bandit-green.

II Court Scene

The minstrel sat
in his chequered song,
feeding his melody,
plucking at
the bone of his lyre:
his head
open, singing.
Up, then down
his nostrils danced
as the official fool,
in garish motley,
sprawled and nodded,
dreaming of oranges.

Across the room,
a nun was trying
to remember her legs.

III January 1649

It has come at last:
The Eternal Regicide
– window a mask
of the temporal night –
It has come:
the moon,
a tambourine husk.
The bile of worms
in a sepulchre's light.

Born, a King rises.
The ingrained wisdom
spends its seed.
Jaws of the lantern
at the steel places
disclose a fallow,
wasted steed.

Forget not, forget not
forget not
powdered ringlet
fool and bowl;
madrigal blossom velvet,
purling basin,
grief and cowl…

'I go from a corruptible
to an incorruptible Crown,
where no disturbance can be;
no disturbance in the world.'

(Father forgive them)

'*Stay for the sign.*'

'I will an' it please Your Majesty.'

(Father forgive them)

Blindly, slowly,
I relax
and bare my shoulders to the axe.

Being an attempt to enter the head of Charles I before it was cut off, during the night before and the morning and afternoon of his execution, 29–30 January 1649.

Easter Incident

'Then came the soldiers, and brake the legs of the first and the other which was crucified with him.
But when they came to Jesus and saw that he was dead already, they brake not his legs.'

St John 19:32–3

When they took him down
his back was blooded with splinters
and his hands and feet were a terrible state.

Joseph of Arimathaea had brought rough linen
and they covered his limp genitals
with care, and his twisted, stiffening face.

The linen was not quite adequate
and his crushed feet stuck out
like a pair of broken, bleeding birds.

They tried moving him away
but no one, it seemed, wanted to touch those appalling feet,
naked and caked with the dust of Jerusalem.

One stared numbly at the rusted, extracted spike
and one shooed away a sniffling dog.
Then one knelt beside him.

They recalled Mary who had bathed and soothed
those sad feet in spikenard and dried them
in a towel of her hair.

With the coarse shawl from her head
she covered them – bound them round
like tender infants to keep them from cold.

Then they lifted him with burning palms,
avoiding that portion of blanket,
red-seeping, where a spear had pierced.

Soldiers, wryly watching them shuffling
and stumbling down the gravel slope,
wondered at the fuss over another dead Jew.

And the stiffened, crippled feet,
cradled in the womb-wet shawl,
rested in the arms of Mary.

Rested, with crusted blood flaking,
awaiting their cleansing in soft waters
as he strolled by the shore of the Tiberian Sea.

Extermination

Two kangaroo feet
that tamped dust pastures;
that danced crust ridges
lifting stark stiff –
rigid.
A rude sign
in the cold beam
that froze it
in museum tableau.

A flesh statue
for the rifles.
The dog bullets
barking out the brain
(brain telling tail
to drive body
– too late –
in wild, sinewed flight)
begrudging its paunch
of mashed grasses.

Blunt axe hacking
off comic-awkward corpse
a useless, nibbling head
and nipping
a long, worm-worthless tail
clean away
from
a cleaned carcass:

Its black-clawed feet
for back-scratchers.
Its fine fur
for wallets
and stuffed Joey-friends;
and flesh
for dog jaws,
dripping happy
on puppy-pet cans.

Lovers we are then

Taking your leg upon me,
your strong haunch holding my hip,
you move three times urgently
in mock entry of me.

I roll you back.
You are so white and shaven.
My tongue moves slowly round
the nerve line in your gum.

In the night I waken
to your moisture and energy.
I extend into your throat,
helpless, as your whore.

I look into your morning face
broken, yet mended and bland.
Every trace of us absorbed there
like water into sand.

Evil Landscape

The bushes comb
like dark curls
down three sides
of the drab house.

A splintered shutter,
once olive green,
bangs leisurely
in the arid wind.

White moths
powder the windows.
A toad fattens
on the grey sill.

Dead children are inside.

All I remember

Your black fur brushed my cheek.
Your tears fell down on me:
I moved my chin inside you.
Your heel was inside me.

My nipples roamed.
Lightly they touched,
like supplicants,
at the convergence of bone.

Those small, pointed bones,
inches above the thigh –
sharp beneath my abdomen
as we part and join.

Something, pulsing, ground against you.
It beat upon your face.
Your lips cracked and opened:
throat, insatiate and dry.

Your tongue moved quickly, quickly.
A lizard in the rocks;
I held and broke you then
like a ripe plum.

Its juice still separates my fingers.

Sydney Excursion

for Helen

In the cab
we went Calloway –
All '30s with eyes closed;
and my pencilled moustache
tickled your powdered nose.

The street went on forever:
an asphalt jumble.
We pointed the way
with lacklustre
lacquerless fingers,
laughing so hard
my nipples ached.

Screw the driver!
All he knows is streets –
while we feel streets ahead:
hayseeds in Haymarket,
collapsing at the drop of a napkin.
And Dixon Street
is just a Yellow Prick Road.

Oh Baby,
we seem to have come
such a long, winding way,
along the shortest possible route,
from jelly-roll to jellyfish.

Raw Pleasure

This night
arousal precedes touch;
your slick labia,
violent pink,
rising urgent to
my gentle – and please – frantic hand.

Always warm musk breath.
Hard pubic knob,
wet bush
and cream belly.

Breast pendulous:
And up to a naked mouth.

Bare bottom burns,
stinging still
above the thick apparatus:
your sweet behind,
tight until spread.

Whisper drunk language,
your skin in orgasm
all night.

For Mike Parr

Thirty Years On

Old
one-armed
riverboat captain
on the stream of consciousness,
gazing, not steering from the bridge.

And me
down below,
swabbing the decks with sad facts,
wiping the floor with history.
Minding my face
while you poke yours in
where it's most wanted:
a face to launch a thousand shifts.

They follow your eyes
around the room,
reading between their lines
for answers to unframed questions.
You squint back at them:
the only Michael Parr in captivity.

But stubbornly
I can't allow time its head,
scanning the horizon instead
for earlier canvases:
a pack of young Tartar faces,
echoes of a voice like spice
or a sound of one hand clapping.

Remembrance

High wind tonight.
The full moon cold
between finger and thumb
like some glossy
cool mint,
going to yellow
with age.

You find it deep
in an old pocket
of some no-longer-worn
jacket,
study it a moment
then toss it away.

My father died
in this narrow,
childhood bed of mine.
I remember the day well.
How he kept trying
to rise:
To throw back the covers
with his wasted arm,
perhaps to wheel
that load of compost
down to the vegetable garden
or fix the bucket handle
or broken toaster
waiting under the house.

and
everything
would
be
all right.

For decades
he had kept
down there
every last bit of string
he found
in one huge ball
that was later tossed away.
And I would press him
firmly
back to the pillow,
saying with a confected smile,
ignoring his imploring,
fearful eyes,
'Now Dad, just rest.'

But he had to get out
anyway at last
to use the bucket,
his distorted body
swaying at the bedside,
where my bookcase
used to be,
as I held
all that was left
of his old genitalia,

a small fragment
of raw rag,
directing the thin
anaemic dribble,
no more than a few drops,
into the green,
calcified bucket.

His great legs
that once
had walked mountains
now useless
as old stumps.
I called my mother
and wife
from the kitchen
to lay him down again;
and when they came,
we had to lift
each one of those
comical, gum-tree legs,
fat as sausages,
leaden with oedema,
heavy as girders,
back onto the dimpled,
green counterpane,
my mother at the foot,
wife at the knee,
me at the thigh –

a small assembly line,
squabbling
in an unseemly panic
of miscommunication.
'Sweet Jesus!
Get it right!'
my mother yelling
in anxiety.

Then Dad's voice cut quietly in
and we stopped,
each with a portion
of leg still in hand,
and turning,
saw on his face
a look of loving
that might well be termed
transfigurative.
'Look at the three of you
all standing together there,'
he smiled kindly
down at us,
his fear broken.
'Just look at the three of you.'
We stood transfixed
by this graceful awareness
of priority
from the dying,
each bearing the dead weight
of that massive leg.

And then we all together
shared one last, small
groundswell of laughter.
It was one of the best things
I ever heard him say
just before
disappearing that night
somewhere
in the deep thickets of sleep.

Years earlier,
well before cool mints,
we would go,
Dad and I,
after dinner
on our ritual hike
up the backyard,
along the diagonal
concrete path,
navigating the clothes line,
to the outdoor dunny
on the hill behind
the house.
Me first,
then him taking longer,
as I sat on the cool step,
the cat sometimes beside me,
with the door open,
Dad straining inside
on a stool,

facing the great panoply
of the night sky,
uncompromised as yet
by electronic haze
or pollution –
the same, changeable moon
up there,
as glowing as a pearl;
the crisp, shiny grains
of innumerable galaxies,
hurtling away
before our searching eyes –
stars long dead
that still shed their light –
and we would always say
that we could see forever.

Song for 2012 in four-part harmony

for Catherine

I

Whenever now it rains
I think of you.
And other times besides…

You bend –
or do you kneel? –
at my crown
and send a sound,
a long and loving note,
deep into my muddled head.
Smooth as a salve,
gliding like a clean,
white blade
in through the scalp
and on towards
my heart and throat.

Around each tone is wrapped
a high cicada ring,
sharp as a celestial bell,
electronic,
inexplicable,
unreal and echoing…

'What did you feel?'
you ask.
A tear rolls to my ear.

There are no words
for what I feel,
nor for what I hear.

II

Within my rib-cage
now has stirred
a very dark and broken bird…

You stand beside me,
hands outstretched.
Inside my lung
a ball of heat
ignites
into a rising sun,
warm as cashmere.
(… And, curling on my lap,
Shakespeare…)

The hands that cup
my chest
seem broad and heavy,
hard and worn.
'It is Jesus,' you smile tenderly.
'They are His hands –
He moves through me.'

Miracles happen inside this door.
And I have felt these hands before.

III

At Ange's place
you bounce.
You hold the cane toads out
to pee.
You laugh. You dance.
You read aloud your poetry.

Your brow is smooth.
Your eye-brows arch in play.
Your Irish eyes are shining
to steal a heart away.

I talk to you incessantly
as though a spring unblocks.
You smile across the room at me
in your Technicolor socks.

And, in that fleeting moment,
it all appears complete:
your chestnut hair
and raven eyes.
Your magic hands.
Your rainbow feet.

IV

Dear Catherine,
I think I love you
best
not so much
in that moment
when the dusty crow is healed.
But rather
in the space
where down you kneel –
though, as yet,
you do not really know
that somehow
you will heal the crow.

In my heart and head
you are singing still.

Wantime Street

At Noosa
you looked new again:
once again new.

At Noosa
everyone spoke:
even the car had its say…

No cats here to get our tongues.
No dogs to bark us down.
Stories tumbled from us
into the listening silence,
our own stories broken among them.

'They came through here, you know.
Let us say
they came right through here –
on their way
from the festive mountains
on a night of full moon
down to the shining coast…'

No cane toads then.
No tall, plastic buckets.
No mobiles or flush toilets.
No Indian tables or African drums.
No Sleeping Siddharthas.

Hundreds, perhaps thousands
of flaming torches
down the dark mountain-sides.
And everyone singing:
a joyous, lilting song,
over and over –
hunters and warriors,
poets and storytellers,
lovers and nurturers,
gatherers,
magicians and healers.

They came, let us say,
right through this house:
Ewen Mundi's people,
The Dulingbara,
and many other,
carrying their young children,
holding their golden hands;
holding their fishing spears and *towrows*;
holding their flaming torches.
Coming, let us even suggest,
right through our bedrooms
in Wantime Street.
And, all the while,
everyone singing.

They pass by us tonight
at full moon,
unheard, as we sit laughing
around the Indian table.
Your four eyes
are like those of schoolgirls.

Can you see them, Catherine?
Can you see them, Ange?
Their tall, straight backs flex
as they pass on through
the acacias and red cedars.
Can you hear them happily singing?
They do not know
that it is Monday
and that the green spotted frog
is now under threat.

Butterflies rise up
in soft, dark clouds around them
from the long grasses.
The dolphin – the *talobilla* –
await their coming.

In the new morning,
the white sands are studded
with cowrie shells.
Soldier crabs scuttle across their feet.
They drum on the water
with open palms and fishing spears,
a familiar rhythm,
their great nets extended,
fishing for millennia
for whiting and fat mullet
with the blue-nosed dolphin
and the blue crane.

Assignation

If all my aches and pains
were poems
and all my memories too,
what a motley bunch of verses
they would be,
without rhyme or reason.
Just like that stunted babble
Of Down's syndrome boys
that day at King's Lynn:
All queuing,
like a disordered anthology,
for the disabled toilet.
All that unwelcome racket–
and no one there
even approaching shoulder-high.

So here I stand again
on that same corner
in Goblin Village,
looking as nonchalant
and unobtrusive as possible –
but nervous inside
with the old uncertainties
as they bustle past me,
glancing in quick suspicion
at this dubious misfit
loitering here,
ignoring the call of nature,
tense with eager eloquence,
waiting for my poem,

late as usual,
to arrive.

Coming towards me
down the stone steps,
her high heels
clipping the hard pavement.
White legs and arms
moving in graceful precision.
Face translucent.
Her viridian dress
glowing like a promise
against the incipient dusk.
Her golden hair,
shimmering beyond words
in the cold, marble light:
unmistakable,
head and shoulders
above the rest.

And seeing me there,
does not smile
or wave
or call out in some familiar voice;
but locks eyes,
sea-green to blue,
and walks purposefully
forward:
an important poem today
(though just words after all –

words stalking a page)
coming straight for me

with a definite fragrance
and an indecipherable expression,
like a book you come upon
suddenly
after a long search,
saying, 'Here I am.
Are you ready
to open me?'
But never
quite
arriving.

On Meeting You

You come here
already clothed in certainty.
I arrive simply
following a hunch.

You burst in:
there is a jungle in your eyes
and an ocean in you;
as I scuttle sideways
along the granular beach
where waves,
cerulean and bold,
crash at my uncertain head
and feet –

Salt sting on skin.
Eyes creased against the sun.

And all around:
the bright,
brightest sky;
the flat, long rocks
away over there,
glistening grey;
the wind shuddering
through the palest green
of grass
on the cool rising…

As if the whole world
were really
this time,
and on this occasion,
expectantly calling.

The end of land.
The beginning of a slow,
unpredictable drowning
into a smiling sea.

If I Lay Naked

If I lay naked in your arms
as the water pipes bled
and the taps dripped
and the toilet ran
and the moon seemed to boil
in the bucket of night
like an alabaster egg…

If I lay naked in your arms
as the words died
and my mouth rested
and my nipples ached
and your body lay
with its fecund strength
on the raddled bed
emitting our smell…

If I lay naked in your arms
with one eye blind
and one eye blurred
and my nostril crushed
against your bigger breast
and your warm hand
coaxing slow interest
from my hooded cock…

If I lay naked in your arms
as the music died
and the clock ticked down
the time left together;
and I heard the lost things
as you fell
brimmed and swollen
beneath my pointed finger...

If I lay naked in your arms
and the hours passed
as our hearts beat
and there were no chores
and no demands
and all pain subsided
and silence fell,
what would we discover
in the soft surrender
of our broken openings?

www.ingramcontent.com/pod-product-compliance
Lightning Source LLC
Chambersburg PA
CBHW070916080526
44589CB00013B/1316